Love. Life. Living.

A Sel

Caroline

Michael Terence
Publishing

First published in paperback by
Michael Terence Publishing in 2021
www.mtp.agency

ISBN 9781800941502

Cover images
Courtesy of Unsplash
www.unsplash.com

Cover design and illustrations

Contents

Life You Crave

Life is sometimes very hard,
You have been dealt a defective card.
You wish that things weren't as they are,
You know all this will leave a scar.
Feels like your heart will never heal,
And real love again you will never feel.
The only way forward is to find some hope,
That you'll change direction and
        end this downward slope.
Take a deep breath, then let it all go;
The pain, the fear, the life you know.
Look up, look forward, be strong, be brave
'Cos within your grasp is the life you crave.

If You Find Love

If you find love, don't take it for granted.
If you find love, hold onto it tight.
If you find love, every day embrace it,
If you find love, treat that love right.
If you find love, never squander its potential,
If you find love, bask in the warmth of its light.
If you find love, treasure each tiny moment.
If you find love, never let it out of your sight.
Because that love is rare and is uplifting,
That love is the most special gift, day and night.
That love can protect you forever,
But turn your back on this love,
And you will lose it for life.

Life Trials

People surprise us every day,
  but often not in a good way.
"How sad is that!" I hear you cry.
  Yes, I know, it makes me sigh.
But do not fret, as it's simply their loss,
Because this is YOUR life, of which you're the boss.
So, let's get real, let's be philosophical,
As often their failings are actually quite comical!
So, smile, hold your head high and stand so very tall,
Because it is YOU that is BIG,
  and them that are small.

How I Love You

Like the swoop of the soaring bird.
The gleam on the glass.
The cooling spray from the sea.
The magic of Christmas.
The glisten of the snow.
The glow of the diamond.
The sweet raindrop on my tongue.
The first taste of sweet honey.
The diving of the dolphin.
The gallop of the horse.
The catching of the fish.
The warm sun after the rain.
This is how I love you.

There and Here

You are there and I am here,
I miss you like crazy, but I won't shed a tear.
Because I know it's not for long,
And soon my heart will sing a different song.
You are my north, my south, my east and west,
And everything else you do it the best.
So let's sit tight, let's bide our time,
Soon enough your heart will beat next to mine.

Time Stands Still

As you leave, it's as though time stands still.
Everything is the same as we say goodbye,
  but then time stands still.
It doesn't slow down or gradually stop,
  it stops suddenly,
With the beating of my heart in that one moment;
When my stricken heart knows you have left.
Time stands still, in that single heartbeat,
  time stands still.
The world will continue to turn,
Even though for me, time stands still.
Until you return, time stands still.
Because you are all of me and I am all of you.
Without one cog, the other cannot turn.
And time stands still.
But when we re-unite,
  the clogs click back together,
And back into life, as suddenly as they stopped.
And in that one euphoric heartbeat,
Time passes once more.

How I Miss You

Like the sun behind the cloud.
Like the bird with the broken wing.
Like the icy wind that cuts in two.
Like the last sweet that is just an empty wrapper.
Like the hungry infant, longing for milk.
Like the homeless dog, craving love.
The roar of the thunder and the
    blaze of the lightning.
The smarting of the bee sting.
The shiver of the chill.
This is how I miss you.

The Wind In the Trees

The wind in the trees.
A movement so pure, so natural.
The wind in the trees,
So free, so escapist.
The wind in the trees,
A ghost, a phantom.
The wind in the trees,
A strength, a force.
The wind in the trees,
So wilful, so wild.
The wind in the trees,
So cool, so uplifting.
The wind in the trees
So bitter, so biting.
The wind in the trees,
So clean, so untarnished.
The wind in the trees
Gives strength, gives focus.
The longing, the yearning,
Of better things to come.
The wind in the trees,
So gently it caresses the leaves.

The wind in the trees,
So ferocious it bends and beats the bow.
Working its way along the branches,
   tugging at the leaves until they surrender,
Scattering and gone from their home forever.
They sway and shimmy,
   dancing to a silent melody only they can hear.
The wind in the trees,
Beginning with a gentle, tinkling melody
   ending in a powerful crescendo.
Repeated in waves, over and over and over
   but still the trees never tire.
Buoyant and proud they dance
   on and on and on…
Until the wind dissipates, the force of nature
   gone as quickly as it arrived.
It departs, swirling away, into thin air,
Leaving the trees peaceful and
   restful once more.
They gently sigh as if in relief,
   recharging from roots to leaves.
They are alone once more, their nonchalant
   dance partner drifting away.
Just the tiniest tips and baby leaves gently toing
   and froing their silent wave goodbye.

And then all is still, a hush and tranquillity
descends once more.
The wind in the trees,
Consumed for the moment,
fulfilled and satiated.
Until, the wind in the trees,
Stirs once more.

Welcome, The Rain

So silently it approaches,
Tiptoeing in the swollen belly overhead.
Creeping and creeping closer,
There will be no escape from it.
It is coming, without doubt, it is coming.
Everything is so still, not one breath of wind
   can you feel on your cheek.
But yet still something approaches.
Somewhere in the distance there is a movement,
Sudden, sharp and direct.
Something falls, dashing to the ground,
knocking against everything in its wake.
Like a cold menacing arrow.
It reaches its target.
You stand motionless, as the beast at large
   gains momentum.
It fires arrow after arrow,
   from its unreachable cache.
Down onto the earth.
In the air too, a change is unfolding.
A cooling sensation descends in the air.

The atmosphere swarms with dampness,
Bearing down on your shoulders,
  mucid, clammy.
You become enveloped in a
  moisture laden blanket.
Look to a leaf,
On its surface glassy droplets are forming,
Like gleaming miniature crystals,
On the next leaf and the next,
  like a silent disease it spreads over everything
  it touches.
The eerie sound from the first attack is replaced
  with the clicking notes,
As the phantom tune plays out,
  crackling to reach its triumphant chorus.
Each note so small and delicate,
But together unbreakable.
An undulation of unrelenting beats,
  it applauds you.
You are surrounded, mesmerized by the
  hypnotising beat.
Building in your ears until it is all you can hear,
  all you can feel, all you can breathe,
Like a lion, it roars.

You rapidly blink away the tiny pearls
lining your eyelashes,
Only to have them replaced once more,
in the passing of a second.
It is futile.
You are now captured, completely at the mercy
of this indelible force.
Welcome, the rain.

Run From love

So, you wear your armour night and day.
Because when might you need it?
Who's to say?
So badly burnt in that fire.
You crave retreat, you need to retire.
The beautiful blossom so sweet and pure,
Is long, long gone, replaced with a vile manure.
Your hopes were high, your spirits too,
A wonderful life was in front of you,
But the trail went cold, almost overnight.
You did all you could, you put up a fight.
But when it's over it's over, when it's gone it's gone.
On the radio plays only a heartbroken song.
The hurt runs deep, piercing your heart.
If only you had known the ending at the start.
But you didn't, so learn for the life anew.
Protect and survive is what you must do.
Run, hide, whatever it takes.
If you're caught out again, so high are the stakes.
So, tread carefully my friend,
As fear grips your heart in its glove.
If ever you feel it start to flutter,
Then run, run from love.

Unstoppable

The waves are building, gaining momentum.
Huge, they loom on the horizon.
Threatening.
Hostile.
Carrying more power than I could ever have,
  or even imagine.
Higher and higher,
Darker and darker.
Stronger and stronger.
Such power it takes my breath away.
Full of menace, full of promise of the inevitable.
Each one crashing down harder
  and faster than the one before.
I am dizzy, swaying with fear.
My heart thunders in my ears.
My legs are like wood, heavy, cumbersome, useless.
I am unable to move,
I am frozen in terror.
But also in awe.
The sea, my long standing nemesis is here now,
  larger than life.
Larger than my life.

This is it;
The final confrontation.
The ending of our story.
But no trace of happiness, no remnant of hope.
We are about to collide.
Like a raging fire, it holds all the power in my
universe at this moment,
And I hold none.
I am completely defenceless.
Nowhere can I run.
No sanctuary I will find.
Just an agonising wait,
  painfully calculating its destination.
And there it is.
The one.
Bigger than anything I have seen in my life.
A dark, towering phantom rising from the ocean.
Surging so high, dragging the clouds along with it.
Coming straight for me.
This is the one.
I will be gone.
It approaches in slow motion.
Although time seems to stop passing,
I know I have no time remaining,
  only incomprehensible fragments of life hang
  before my eyes.

My time is done.
My pulse is in overdrive.
I cannot drag my eyes from its majestic crest.
Like a ravenous eagle in flight,
About to swoop to take its cowering prey.
Gasping I know I must take the breath of my life
Quick! A deep, long, gasping breath fills me,
But I feel hollow.
Nothing. A void about to be erased.
Taken by the undertow.
The smell hits me, filling my nostrils.
Taking over every sense of my being.
The salty freshness gone,
The stench of rotting fish,
Decaying seaweed,
I am overwhelmed.
Then the rolling begins,
Like the final act of this macabre play.
The vast, grey volume of movement.
Folding down.
Rolling, lurching, pitching forward.
Effortlessly taking all in its wake.
Unstoppable.
I crouch.
Lungs expanded further than they should
ever have to stretch.

Crammed with my final breath, my final hope.
The rest of me is crunched, hunched as tight as I can.
And I fall into a black hole.
Darkness.
This is the one.
This is definitely the one.
The one to take me under.
Under, under until I am gone.

The Airport

You have entered the airport,
What could be worse?
Across it all, you must transverse.
Pushing and shoving, weaving in and out.
Chaos reigns here, there is no doubt.
Where are the trolleys?
   What was your flight number?
To the correct check-in desk,
You finally lumber.
Nothing is moving, just a huge human snake,
Slithering forwards, forever it takes.
Then like the sun after the rain,
   a new face appears.
Taking your baggage,
Erasing your fears.
But oh no, what's that? My case is too heavy?
And I am forced to pay the airline levy.
Next goal, get your passport checked again.
Which way should I go? Get in which lane?
You choose the middle, it doesn't look too bad.
Then you end up behind a beer swilling lad.

He ricochets around the straights and bends,
Catching up to all his beer swilling friends.
Finally the x-ray machine,
all space age and strange.
It's off with your shoes, belt and loose change.
Your hand luggage passed, hip hip hurray!
You scrabble to take your effects out of the tray.
But wait, someone in uniform tells you to stop.
She opens your bag and finds
the nail scissors on top.
Oh goodness I'm sorry, I always forget those!
And into her bucket the offending items goes.
You gather your belongings and self esteem
And what lays ahead makes you beam.
Glossy gadget shops and cafes galore,
You must pass through duty-free,
it is the airport law!
You wait in line for coffee,
or maybe something stronger,
Cos you really aren't sure you can take
this much longer.
Huge coffee seen off, let's check boarding news.
You stare at the screen,
wondering where are the loos?
Flipping heck you start to panic.
This run to gate 25 is going to be manic!

Why is my plane parked so far away?
If I'd know this before,
I would have checked in yesterday!
So off you lurch to the challenge ahead,
Wishing you were already beachside on a sunbed.
You reach the gate breathless and red in the face.
But now your boarding card has vanished
without trace.
Your bag seems to be the Bermuda triangle,
You wonder out loud,
which excuse you can wangle.
One last ditch attempt, you check all around,
And there in your pocket it is finally found.
You swan through the gate, freedom at last!
The headless chicken act, a thing of the past.
Ecstatic euphoria descends on you then,
Until you realise, it's just 7 days
until you hit the airport again.

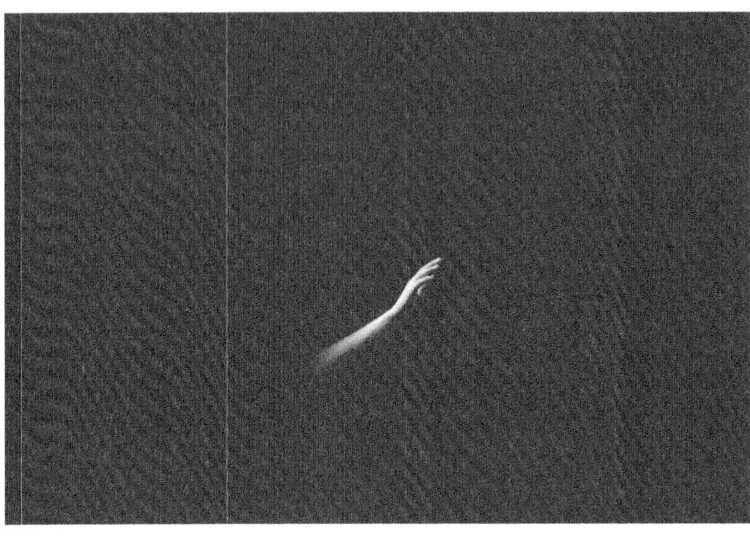

Lies and Deceit

Lies and deceit.
The secrets we keep.
The skeletons that dangle and rattle and jangle.
The darkness we inhabit,
To keep the light on.
Black corners of our minds,
Where we leave the bad stuff behind.
We smile, we promise,
We love, we care.
But meanwhile there is a monster back there.
The deception and fraud,
The twisted the tainted.
Nothing like the outside picture
we have painted.
The lies and deceit,
The secrets we keep.
It will drive us under,
Lives ripped asunder.
Secrets of the heart,
Deep and dark.

Lock them away,
Try to keep them at bay.
Lies and deceit,
The secrets we keep.
No matter what you do
They will define you.

Behind Closed Doors

Behind closed doors,
Who knows what occurs?
Who knows what stirs?
Who can say?
The mundane, the insane,
The lives unknown.
Clues can be found,
But secrets are bound.
Tied to each door,
Of which there's no key.
No way in and no way to see.
The trail impassable,
The destination impenetrable.
The darkness and light,
And screams in the night.
A comedy, soap opera, crime and
punishment all rolled into one,
Every fantasy, reality under the sun.
Behind closed doors,
There are no laws,
And what we don't know can't hurt us.

Five Long Weeks of Covid-19 (Part I)

Five long weeks of Covid-19,
So I'd like to ask "How have you been?".
Toilet roll wars seem to have finished.
But the anti-bac warriors have not diminished!
Squish that gel, swoosh those wipes,
and spray, spray, spray!
As long as you keep those bloody germs away.
Netflix rules and Amazon Prime,
Crikey there's so much TV time.
Let's look in the supermarket, what's occurring?
Deliveries are in and the stockroom is stirring.
If there're no tinned tomatoes
for your bolognese,
Hang on, chill out, it's just a phase.
Wine, chocolate, pizza is all still there,
So sod it if the tinned shelves are bare!
The sun was shining, the weather was hot,
People carried on like lockdown forgot.

Now it's cloudy, pouring at times,
Oh well I guess they'll be less fines.
There's always Joe Wicks on your TV,
Jump about the lounge and shake your booty!
Google classroom is all maxed out.
There are lots of trainee teachers about.
Maths, English, science OMG! They wail,
When it gets too much, do a nature trail.
Are you eating your weight in crisps and snacks?
For this we can't find any life hacks!
Food, food, glorious food,
If nothing else, it helps your low mood.
Sales for alcohol must have gone up,
In between eating, it's sup, sup, sup!
Every day is a bad hair disaster.
Hairdressers are in hiding,
So it's growing faster.
No longer can we pop to our local salons,
To coif up the hair or buff the talons.
So now we all look like Boris from number 10,
Who seems to have lost his comb again.
I don't think his barber is missing him,
It's been years since he did anything.
But poor ol' Boris has been through the mill,
Ended up in intensive care as he was so ill.

Now his partner has popped their wee sprog,
So it's all systems go and back to his job.
We wait to see what's next up his sleeve,
Thank god he's not taking paternity leave.
So for the rest of us mere mortals
  it's on with lockdown.
In villages, cities, boroughs and towns.
So keep up the good work, fight the good fight.
Eventually we'll be through this darkness
  and into the light.

Play to Win

Play to win,
In the game of life that you're in.
When the going gets hard,
Don't let down your guard.
Through the rough and the smooth,
There is so much to prove.
Act like you've already won,
Before its even begun.
You are a winner through and through,
No one can take that from you.
Fight as hard as you must,
To watch them all bite the dust.
The only real enemy,
Is the one within.
When he starts to shout,
Do not listen to him.
Drown out your fears,
And fight, fight, fight.
Through the blood sweat and tears,
With all of your might.

Take the knocks along the way,
You can't win every day.
But play you must,
It's your all or bust.
So play to win,
You'd be a fool not to do.
This game of life,
Don't let it beat you.

My Ocean

So concealing,
But so intimate.
So dangerous,
But so inviting.
So powerful,
But so gentle.
So brackish,
But so delicious.
So transparent,
But so unknown.
So pure,
But so tainted.
So encapsulating,
But so releasing.
So tranquil,
But so turbulent.
So illuminated,
But oh so dark.

So energising,
And yet so tiring.
So certain,
But so dynamic.
So shared,
And yet so mine.

The Biggest Mystery

My friend,
My foe,
My ebb,
My flow.
My saviour,
My rival,
My love,
My idol.
My strength,
My weakness,
My hope,
My bleakness.
My courage,
My fear,
My far,
My near.
My ally,
My opposition,
My proof,
My supposition.

My whole,
My broken,
My silence,
My spoken.
My together,
My alone,
My softness,
My stone.
My black,
My white,
My wrong,
My right.
My sickness,
My health,
My poverty,
My wealth.
For all that is good,
There is that is bad.
For all that makes me happy
Makes me so sad.
How can a soul be so complex?
You leave me calm,
You leave me vexed.
I need to know who you can truly be.
But I will never know,
You are the biggest mystery.

People

People are the strangest creatures.
Techni colour beings,
Never black and white.
A multitude of shades of grey.
A spectrum so vast it is blinding.
People are the strangest creatures.
There are the chameleons.
Ever changing as if played by
  a rainbow keyboard.
Red, green, yellow, blue,
Every single hue.
People are the strangest creatures.
They radiate warmth.
Then they blast cold.
They are kind.
They are cruel.
They are polite.
They are rude.
They sing and dance and yell like thunder!
And then they whisper.
Oh the whispering!
People are the strangest creatures.

The secret codes they use to
   murmur and mumble.
Each one unique, complex,
   mixed-up and tortuous.
Twisting and winding like vicious
   serpents around your ears.
Never will you ever fathom it out,
   this undecipherable program.
Never will you penetrate the poison.
You must resist this witch-hunt!
People are the strangest creatures.
They change with the wind.
Blowing hot.
Blowing cold.
Blowing north.
Blowing south.
People like that,
They can just blow away.

If Only

Eyes wide and innocent.
And oh, so very bright.
Even in the darkness,
They radiate such light.
Their little hearts full of goodness.
Their minds so sweet and pure.
You pray that to the other side,
  evil will never, ever lure.
Always only the good they see,
If only the world, could this way be.
When does this change as we age?
It is something that is so hard to gauge.
Suddenly we start to fear,
The unknown of things both far and near.
If only our hearts could stay childlike,
The world would be such a different sight.

The Wings of Song

Black can be so black.
The richest ebony.
The darkest imagination.
The deepest abyss.
Of loneliness, wretchedness and despair.
All hope is fractured.
All light is gone.
Not a spark.
Not even a fleck of dust.
Your soul is waning, almost extinguished.
You are swallowed whole, consumed by this
 infinite cavern of darkness.
The pressure bears down, unabating, merciless.
Imprisoning you with its demon serpents,
Wrapping and writhing around your limbs.
Tighter still, they cling to your mind
 and suppress your soul.
To your very core,
They are grinding, pulling and twisting
 everything that you are
And everything you yearn to be.
Solid and surrounding.

Suffocating.
Enclosing.
Darkness sucks away at your life,
Your very being.
Your actual mortality.
You try to lift yourself away,
To somewhere, anywhere.
You don't want this to be the end.
Clawing and scratching you fight to find a
crevice or foothold that isn't there.
Isn't there until…
A sudden beacon in front of your eyes,
You remember the one thing which saved you,
Saved you, the last time the darkness descended.
Affirming you are not beaten yet.
You will not go quietly.
You grapple for the only weapon you have,
Pulling the trigger marked "PLAY".
Your senses ignite.
You breathe.
Still you breathe!
You feel the rush of pure, fresh oxygen
Flooding in.
Expelling out.
All is not gone.

The very life of you which felt like
it was leaving, pauses.
And turns around.
And smiles at you.
And there it is.
The retaliation begins.
The notes float down, filling the first bar.
Then the next and the next.
Held by velvet measures that soothe
your weary soul.
And fills your heart with an invincible hope.
The beats and bars swell and thrive,
Until they gain wings.
Beautiful, breathtaking wings.
You take flight,
Ascending higher and higher with each heroic beat.
Each note lifts you further from the darkness,
Elevating you on their glittering girders of gold
Flanked by diamonds pulleys
Navigated only by your soul.
The black hole fades to grey,
Now, not even a pin prick on your universe.
The song flourishes into a captivating
bridge of iridescence,
Taking you to its euphoric climax,
You reach the sparkling summit of liberation.

But you don't descend.
Only ascend some more,
The music in complete charge of your elevation.
Floating in an aural sea of the most
 vibrant kaleidoscopic hues
You drink in the liquid golds and silvers.
Molten, they cascade through your atmosphere,
Showering you in rejuvenation.
Renewed, you sail ever upwards.
Out of the black,
Into the blue.
Let the blackness fade out, but never the music.
And may your soul be forever entwined
 to the wings of song.

Covid-19
(Part II)

Eight more long weeks of Covid-19,
And I'd like to ask, how have you been?
Things have started moving, the wheels are turning.
And for some, a desire to get back to the pub is burning!
For you, did all those lockdown weeks fly?
Look now it's almost 4th July!
Hip, hip, hurrah! I hear you cry.
Landlords prepare to have your kegs drunk dry!
For some a foreign holiday is now in sight,
So get web surfing and find a flight.
Some exercise resolutions fell at the wayside.
We tried on our jeans and blubbed and cried.
At full capacity are some waistbands,
Primark has reopened and they are rubbing their hands.
For some, it was back to work as normal,
Home offices shut down
　　and things were more formal.
People are out more doing their daily tasks.

Some are sporting matching gloves and masks.
Home schooling is still full throttle,
More than a few teachers are hitting the bottle.
Hardly surprising, it's a stressful way to live.
Under all the current pressure,
Something has to give.
Delivery drivers have grafted non-stop
It's definitely no job for a workshy fop!
More parcels & packages than you have ever seen.
Ding dong, on the doorstep,
The courier has been.
DIY stores have taken a hit.
Everyone needing their home improvement kit.
What else can we do to while away the hours?
Painting, grouting and feeding the flowers.
The weather was hot, the beaches were packed,
Whoever was on litter duty,
Should definitely be sacked.
The air is cleaner,
The rivers are too.
But the beaches are filthy,
Someone even dug their own loo!
This whole lockdown business,
Is a mixed bag all right.
Some folk are calmer,
Some just want to fight.

Boris from number 10 is still hanging in there.
Declared his best friends could re-open
The ones that do hair.
This is great news for those of us
    who resemble a scarecrow.
But how long will it take to get an appointment?
We would really love to know!
Must not forget our wonderful NHS.
How hard it's all been, is anyone's guess.
The Thursday night round of applause,
They deserve so much more for their key cause.
So thank you from us, for all you have done.
To each employee, every single one.
For all the frontline crew, Police and Teachers too,
In these exceptional times,
We salute you.

Covid-19 (Part III)

So our first Covid Christmas is almost here,
And generally speaking there isn't much cheer.
We've all received a gift we have never had before.
Tier 1, 2 or 3, for some poor sods it's tier 4.
Rules and regulations, and bubbles galore,
Fines if we break them, says the voice of the law.
Who to have around the table on Christmas Day?
It's like Russian roulette:
        who can come, who's kept at bay?
At least the dilemma of what to give has
        been taken away,
We know what they'll be opening on
        this Christmas Day.
Sanitiser, loo roll, or a fancy face mask,
Shopping made easy,
We don't need to ask.
The trees are up and the lights are glowing
But stress hangs in the air, and the sense
        of not knowing.

What will 2021 hold in store?
Please no more Covid, we can't take anymore.
The vaccine was created and is being offered around,
But the naysayers are shouting,
        many faults they have found.
To me, it is progress, a hope, a way out.
But "it's terribly flawed!" I have heard many shout.
The rumours circulate and the tension grows
What do we do, who bloody knows.
But stay hopeful, look forward, there will be an end,
And with luck, it will come,
        before we go 'round the bend.
Eat the Turkey, the chocs and the mince pies
Drink wine or whisky to help drown out the lies.
For life is short and for some poor souls,
Covid took their chance to reach their goals.
So come what may,
In whatever shape or form.
Christmas Day will be very different from the norm.
But in every home, whether near or far,
We all pray for the same, whoever we are.
The same wish will be whispered,
        whether you are big or small,
For an end to Covid-19,
Once and for all.

The Story of Sunrise

In the early stillness,
Something stirs beyond.
From the heart of this planet,
Breathtaking colours do abscond.
Burning so intense.
The illumination immense.
A core of white,
Transmits an abundance of light.
Liquid gold floods the sky.
We do not need to reason why;
A fluorescence to show the way.
A signal, it's time to start our day.
Sunrise, sunrise,
Open your eyes.
Or else you will miss,
This light show of bliss.
Ascending now, it gathers pace.
Although the sky is vast,
It fills the space.
With the richest colours, of sunken gold,
It proudly radiates its strength;
So let the story of sunrise unfold.

The World of the Bunny

So welcome to the world of the bunny
As long as there is hay
It's always sunny.
Scratching and foraging
All around.
If there is food down there
It will be found!
Noses twitch,
As ears listen
Tails are bobbing
And bright eyes glisten.
What's the human giving us now?
Chew sticks, carrot, I think it's apple?
Oh wow, wow, wow.
Straight down the hatch
Didn't mean to snatch!
If you let you hand linger
I might nip your finger!
It's not that I'm in a bad mood
Just that I thought it was food!
I love to scratch, and chew and dig.

And have a good old knaw
    on an apple tree twig.
I'm fast, I'm clever, and so agile.
Just watch me binky,
And I'll watch you smile!
My favourite thing in the world is hay
To eat, to poop on, or to just lay.
Speaking of poop, to keep you in the loop.
Of those little brown gifts,
There will be piles.
Because we are champion poopers
Oh yes, by miles!
We even chew
When we're on the loo.
Really? I hear you asking
Yes! It's bunny multi tasking.
We love you humans, because you give us food
But we love hay more
Just being honest, not rude!

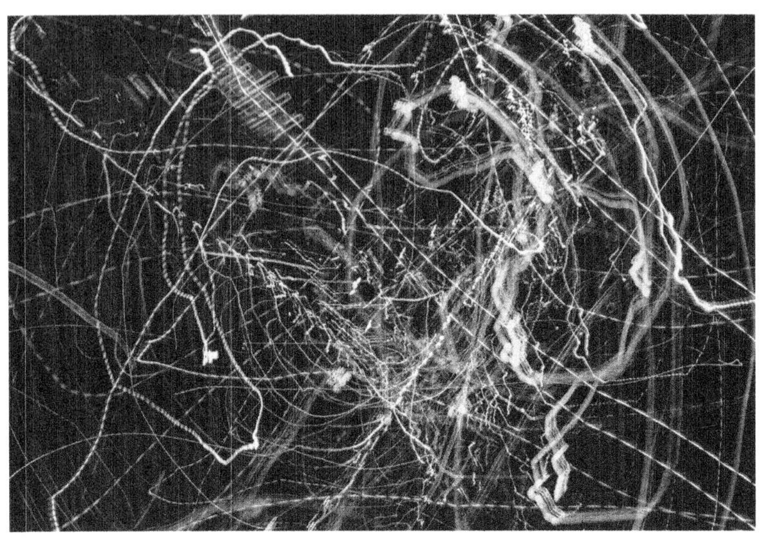

Sweet Dreams

The places.
The faces.
The vivid and the blurred.
A stranger we know,
Speaks concisely,
Speaks slurred.
The things we do,
So real at the time.
Can be completely innocent,
Or can be the worst crime.
As we slumber and as we sleep,
Our thoughts run wild,
And oh so deep.
Twisted serpents in our minds,
Come out to play, at bedtime.
Things you never knew,
Suddenly confront you.
Things you've tried to forget,
Become even more ingrained yet.
You can run and hide,
But like your shadow,
Dreams will stay by your side.

Taunting and teasing.
Pleasant and pleasing.
Whatever comes to you,
Your mind is working through.
In REM,
You're at it again.
Into another world,
You are involuntarily hurled.
The dark recesses of your mind
God knows what your'll find.
When we all sleep,
Nothing is as it seems.
So goodnight, sleep tight,
I pray you have sweet dreams.

Those Repping Days

Written by Caroline Hill, an ex-rep and proud of it.

Those repping days, oh those repping days!
We remember the era in so many ways.
The good, the bad and the downright vile,
Made us angry, made us swear,
    but mostly laugh our tits off and smile!
The all-nighters on the airport run,
Followed by piss-ups 'till dawn,
It had to be done!
For hours on end, to the airport they came in droves,
How we stood and kept smiling God only knows.
Finally rounded up and on the way to resort,
Rest stop? asks the driver
'No chance! Put your foot down!'
    you hear us retort.
Cos so tight is this schedule I really must keep,
By my reckoning, I might make 3 hours sleep.
Then roll outta bed, leg it to your first hotel,
They are queuing with complaints,
Oh crapping hell.

Your hotel is a doss hole and I don't give a fig,
So get ticking that booking form
Make my spend per head nice n big!
Customer service top of our list?
Do me a favour, it's make money first
    and second get pissed!
I showed up today, though I'm
    bloody cream-crackered,
So I don't give a toss if your aircon is knackered.
Later it's time for that legend, that was Bar Crawl,
These were the nights when we saw it all.
The vomit, the domestics, and the secrets came out,
Coach leaving in ten! I hear the rep shout.
Oh dear it seems I have less bodies
    than when I started,
Bugger me this repping lark is not
    for the faint hearted.
Never mind, now the real fun begins,
Get the shots lined up,
Time for a night full of sins!
The mindless liaisons, and meaningless shagging,
In our defence, the locals were usually gagging!
Tomorrow seems so far away,
And those 'feckin' rehearsals for caberet.

Those repping days, oh those repping days.
We remember that era in so many ways.
A lifetime ago, but forever carved on your mind.
The memories made and the friends left behind.
Once a rep, always a rep in your heart,
You want more stories?
OMG, where do I start!!!

The Clutches of Lockdown

Release me from the clutches of lockdown,
Let me smile once more, and lose this frown.
Release me from the clutches of lockdown,
Let me travel from place to place,
And town to town.
Let me stand where I want, and please let me sit,
Let us once more, be close-knit.
Let me embrace loved ones, both far and near.
Let us share our lives, without the fear.
Let us mix and mingle,
With spines that tingle,
As escapades come thick and fast,
Making memories that are meant to last.
Give the frontline angels, their ultimate respite,
Conclude the toil and sweat, of both day and night.
May the cabin crew greet me, with a dazzling smile,
As I take my seat, whether window or aisle.
Let the children party, with candles on cake,
Let them interact, and new friends make.
Oh lockdown, lockdown, just leave me be!
Bring me back to life,
Let me live carefree.

Where Does Love Go When It Dies?

Where does love go when it dies?
Where does the light go when it leaves your eyes?
When your spirit is broken,
There is such pain, but unspoken.
Locked up tight inside, you bear its heavy load,
Afraid one day a tiny leak could fatally implode.
A heart that's crushed,
But a tongue that stays hushed.
Unspeakable depths in the ice-cold dark,
Barren, empty, worthless, stark.
When faith absconds, breaking all it's bonds,
Never ever to return, this lesson you learn;
Don't trust,
Don't give,
Don't love,
But therefore don't live?
A heart that's hollow, a burnt out shell,
Oh that's the testament to love's bittersweet hell.

When the light goes out, it's gone forever.
To the heart strings, you definitely did sever.
Where does love go when it dies?
A question I can only ever surmise.

Erasure

If I erase the past,
Will the effect last?
Or just delete some minutes, hours or a day?
Will the hurt finally go away?
Will it change my outlook?
Will it replace all that the hurt took?
Will my weary soul breathe once more?
Will it make my heart less raw?
Will I see with brighter eyes?
The good and the potential staring me in the eyes?
We say the past creates who we are,
An indication we have come so far.
I believe this is true, but if only we knew.
The effect of the past, forever will last.
It can make us strong, but oh so weak,
Especially when we do not speak.
Of things that bit, and stung and faults did make,
Of things we bore and cannot shake.
And I know that maybe no-one can see,
But everywhere I go, heartbreak walks with me.

We are hand in hand,
Though all unplanned!
So if I erase the past, will heartbreak leave me be?
Drop my hand and set me free?

Do Not Fear the Affray

Cold and dark
Barren and stark.
I shiver.
As I stand by the stagnant river.
Pewter skies push down on me
I search for an escape
But none I see.
Trees rise like phantom shapes
Menacing, they make these haunting landscapes.
Shivers wash down my hunched up spine
My breath is ragged and out of time.
What is scaring me now, I do not know,
And yet I feel this circling foe.
Sharp, wet rock, on which I stand,
Unbalances me and sends out
        my grasping hand.
I reach into the emptiness, the cold space,
        the abyss.

I am filled with uncertainty, but I know just this.
Life peaks and troughs, with highs and lows,
Nothing ever stays the same,
Constantly it flows.
As I raise my eyes, something is shifting.
The clouds are thinning, the gloom is lifting.
Sweeter air my lungs inhale,
And finally sun, albeit wan and pale.
My heart enlivened, my soul revived.
From the uncertainty,
I stand, survived.
The river babbles, I hear it say;
When your life loses harmony,
Do not fear the affray.

Adrift

Adrift once more
For a distant shore.
Oceans of the truest blue
And within them, creatures of every hue.
As far as my eye can see,
That is where I want to be.
The coldest peak or the warmest sand,
Take me there,
To that unknown land.
Lush green tropics, with beady eyes,
Will give me perspective, cut me down to size.
Steer my tiny world, to one so vast,
Push my boat from the dock and away I'll cast.
Vibrant fruits and pungent spice,
Mouth-watering aromas that will entice.
Every culture and every creed,
Pastures new to satiate my greed.
From bustling cities to barren land,
Let me breathe the air,
Run fingers through the sand.
Gushing waterfalls draw me near,
Salty oceans wash away my fear.

Fresh new faces at every turn,
From them so much I want to learn.
Let me run, and let me fly,
From hidden caves, to way up high.
Like a bird, I want to soar,
From cloudless skies,
To the ocean's floor.
Let the waves engulf me with their power,
Though in awe, I will not cower.
Soul and senses revitalised,
From all the magic before my eyes.
So there I go, adrift once more,
Pushing through discovery's door.

Marital Status

What is your marital status,
	your conjugal position?
A question loaded with supposition.
We tick the box, and the box can't lie,
But with every tick there is much more
	than meets the eye.
Single, but loving to mingle.
Joining yet another dating website,
Swiping left, and swiping right.
Or single much planned,
An island on which no one is welcome to land.
When the past has cast a heart of stone,
And these fragile souls, seek to be alone.
Divorced or apart,
For an essential fresh start.
Affairs of the heart,
Can tear us apart.
A loveless state,
Can quickly turn to hate.
Separated and divided,
But still undecided.

The unbidden end from being widowed,
Through a terrible loss, a cruel fate bestowed.
Or this status is one that can relieve,
Not always unwelcome
Depending on what you perceive.
Matrimony: A million shades of grey
Though started out white,
On the wedding day.
Still married through choice,
Where you still have a voice.
Married for convenience,
Can mean much less lenience.
Married but can't really recall why,
The faraway past, happy days gone by.
The ones willing to put the work in,
The reluctant ones, who live in sin.
Hardly novel, in fact the most popular way,
To have a relationship, in our modern day.
Though check the statistics, and they will say,
To be most fulfilled, marriage is the best way.
Marginally topping the polls,
Of those relationship goals.
So whatever your status,
        and which box you may be,
I send you contentment or the courage
        to set yourself free.

Jack Frost

Under the street light,
Like glitter it falls.
I hear him approach,
And softly he calls.
His faithful accomplices, serve him well,
For Jack Frost has now cast his spell.
Tiny at first,
Then larger they swell.
Pure white flakes,
From his icy hell.
They swirl and twirl their frozen dance,
Will you step outside?
Will you take your chance?
For soon the ground is overcome,
Layer upon layer, from the very first one.
The icy flakes of crystal white,
Secretly fall while you sleep curled up tight.
Silent, silent Jack Frost creeps on,
By morning all that looks normal will be gone.
A swathe of frosty landscape, glistening bright,
Will greet us all in the morning light.

Unwavering, determined,
Jack continues his work,
For him the icicles are but perks.
Once all is white, much pride he'll take,
When he surveys the landscape,
The icing on his cake.
Crisp, fresh and oh so cold,
The story of Jack Frost,
Will never get old.

Summer Days

Across the meadow,
Floats a rippled haze.
Oh how I love these summer days!
The crickets chirp,
And the bees buzz,
From petal to petal,
Goes their stripey fuzz.
The grass is warm and smells so sweet,
I kick off my shoes and wiggle my feet.
Bathed by the sun,
Even though my work's not done.
I feel hazy and calm,
From the summer day's balm.
Lazy and carefree,
I just want to be.
The slightest breeze lifts my hair
Taking with it, my final care.
A day like this,
Is beyond pure bliss!
Into the endless cobalt blue I gaze,
Oh how I love these summer days.

Things I've Learnt in Lockdown

Cherish every moment with loved ones and friends,
Make the most of each moment, before it ends.
Include a hairdresser for your bubble,
Or you'll be guaranteed countless 'bad hair' trouble!
Wash your hands and wear a mask,
'Cos this is really not much to ask.
If you eat a bit too much and put on weight,
Find an exercise you love, it's never too late.
If the "must have" item is sold out
No need to scream and shout.
Search the web for your desired loot,
There will always be a substitute.
Be extra kind, in words and deed,
For this small request, we all have the same need.
Don't watch the news unless it's essential,
Otherwise to go crackers, there is great potential!
A hug, an embrace or a kiss,
These things I know, I really miss.

Home schooling, what a task!
Only approach with a full hip flask!
I was already proud of our NHS,
But now words escape me, so give it your best guess!
Life, love and and just living,
All the things we hold dear.
Lockdown has taught me to be brave,
And live without fear.

Available worldwide from Amazon

www.mtp.agency

mtp.agency

@mtp_agency

Printed in Great Britain
by Amazon

60825195R00058